CONTENTS

The Daily Grind 7
    Finding the miraulous in the mundane

Home Sweet Home 33
    The blessings at your doorstep

The Little Things 61
    Everyday unsung treasures

Stopping to Smell the Roses 99
    Refresing detours from the beaten path

Finding the Silver Lining 131
    Recognizing the good in everything

Scripture Index 157

Give
Thanks

*Powerful Prayers for
Everyday Blessings*

BARBOUR
PUBLISHING

© 2010 by Barbour Publishing, Inc.

ISBN 978-1-60260-831-3

Written by Joanna Jeffries.

Published by Barbour Publishing, Inc., P.O. Box 719, Uhrichsville, Ohio 44683, www.barbourbooks.com

Our mission is to publish and distribute inspirational products offering exceptional value and biblical encouragement to the masses.

Printed in the United States of America.

INTRODUCTION

Perhaps one of the most difficult Christian teachings to put into practice comes from Paul in his first letter to the Thessalonians: "Rejoice always; pray without ceasing; in everything give thanks."

At face value, it seems like a simple command to carry out. After all, it's so easy to give joyful thanks for the big, obvious blessings that our generous God has bestowed on us—our families, our homes, our freedom, and our prosperity. But how often do we send up praise for the unassuming gifts of laundry, traffic jams, and laugh lines? In their own way, these blessings in disguise truly reveal the nonstop, intimate nature of the love our Father seeks to shower upon His beloved children. But every day we overlook a multitude of God's richest gifts, taking them for granted and writing them off as inconvenient and mundane.

This book is designed to challenge you to open your eyes and recognize the praiseworthy blessings that are around every corner. Divided into convenient sections for browsing, you'll find prayers on everything from the express checkout line and sleepless nights to daylight savings time and bathroom scales—all offering a joyful new perspective that will leave you in awe of our God's marvelous goodness.

So don't waste another moment—*Give Thanks*!

The Daily Grind

Finding the miraculous in the mundane

Paper Cuts

• • • • • •

Father, it's amazing that something as small as a paper cut can be so painful. Thank You for this reminder that when one part of the body is in pain, the whole body suffers. Help me stay positive and apply this principle to my daily life.

Budgeting Wisely

• • • • • •

Lord, there are so many ways to spend money that it can be overwhelming, but I thank You for giving me so many choices. Thank You for the promise of wisdom when I ask for it and for entrusting this money to me. Help me spend it in a way that honors You.

Learning a New Skill

• • • • • •

Father, it's hard to learn a new skill. I sometimes feel inept and unable when I try something new. Thank You for the gift of patience as I learn. I am grateful that You have given me everything I need to succeed.

Facing a Learning Challenge

• • • • • •

Dear Father, I feel frustrated when I cannot do something I think I should be able to do. It's times like these when I am most grateful for the special talents and abilities You have given especially to me. Thank You for Your calming presence. Help me slow down and trust that all things are possible through You.

Since everything God created is good,
we should not reject any of it
but receive it with thanks.

1 TIMOTHY 4:4 NLT

Sick with a Cold

• • • • • •

Lord, I hate being sick. How could I ever take feeling well for granted? I'm miserable right now, but I know I'll be back to normal soon. Thank You for creating my body with the blessed ability to heal itself.

Working Out

• • • • • •

Lord, today is one of those days when the couch is looking a whole lot more tempting than my workout routine. . . . Sometimes it's hard to get motivated, but I know regular exercise will honor my body—Your temple. Thank You for giving me a body that is so fearfully and wonderfully made and the awesome responsibility that comes with it.

First Day of School

• • • • • •

Lord, the first day can be so intimidating. As a new school year begins, help me set goals with You in mind. Despite the uncertainty, I am thankful for this opportunity to begin anew and learn in abundance.

Going to the Dentist

• • • • • •

Father, I certainly dread all those instruments and drills. But as much as I dislike going to the dentist, I know it's a necessary discomfort that I would be at a loss without. Thank You for making dental care available to me, and give me the resolve to take advantage of it.

The LORD directs the steps of the godly.
He delights in every detail of their lives.

PSALM 37:23 NLT

A New Boss

• • • • • •

Lord, adjusting to a new boss isn't always easy,
and though I may be apprehensive, I thank You
for this new leader. Thank You for all the people
of authority You have placed in my life. Help me
follow their guidance and make this person's job
easier by doing mine well.

A New Co-Worker

• • • • • •

Father, thank You for a new co-worker. I know
our paths have not crossed by accident. As I get to
know them, help me share with them Your light
and Your love.

Turning Off the Lights for the Night

• • • • • •

Heavenly Father, another day is done. Thank You for the things I accomplished today with Your help, and thank You for abiding with me as I sleep.

First Day Back from Vacation

• • • • • •

Lord, as hard as it is to come back from vacation, thank You for the time to rest, relax, and rejuvenate. Thank You for a routine to come back to. Thank You for the importance You place on rest and for continuing to guide me in making it a priority.

Rejoice always; pray without ceasing;
in everything give thanks; for this is
God's will for you in Christ Jesus.
1 THESSALONIANS 5:16–18 NASB

April 15

• • • • • •

Dear Father, paying taxes often feels like an enormous burden, but help me to be grateful for the blessings my tax dollars provide—good roads, libraries, education. Thank You for the privileges of living in a wealthy country.

Standing in Line at the DMV

• • • • • •

Lord, when it comes to standing in line, the line at the DMV has to be the longest. Thank You for the gift of patience, and help me keep this time spent waiting in perspective. It's such a privilege to be able to transport myself from one place to another, and this is but a small price to pay for that freedom.

While on Hold

• • • • • •

I have such a hard time waiting for things, Lord,
but I'm grateful for this reminder that I'm not at
the center of the universe—You are. Thank You,
Father, for never putting me on hold.

My Third Cup of Coffee

• • • • • •

Thank heaven for coffee! It's definitely a three-
cup kind of day, Father. . . . Help my body utilize
this caffeine and focus on the task at hand.

*Don't worry about anything; instead,
pray about everything. Tell God what you need,
and thank him for all he has done.*

PHILIPPIANS 4:6 NLT

Waiting on a Download

• • • • • •

Father, I've become so spoiled by lightning-fast
results: fast food, instant messages, and high-
speed Internet. Thank You for this technology
that makes my daily life more convenient—
I know it's unreasonable to expect everything
instantaneously. Your triumphant return is
especially worth the wait.

Checking E-Mail

• • • • • •

Sometimes I wish I could just turn off my e-mail,
Lord. So many messages! Some days they seem
never ending. Deep down, though, I know I'm
grateful for this speedy communication—even if
it means an extra hour at the office.

No Parking Spots Up Front

• • • • • •

You have blessed me with two capable legs, Lord—
so why do I avoid putting them to good use? I
dread the spot at the back of the lot, but I know
the extra little bit of exercise will benefit me.

When the Day Drags

• • • • • •

Thank You for this uneventful day, Lord. I may
feel tempted to steal an anxious glance at the
clock, but I'm grateful for every moment, no matter how slowly they seem to pass. I cherish this
calm day because only You know what tomorrow
will bring.

He calms the storm, so that its waves are still.

PSALM 107:29 NKJV

Running to the Convenience Store

• • • • • •

I can be so forgetful sometimes, Lord!
Though I'm bothered that I need to run back
to the store, I'm grateful that I have convenient
places to turn. In the same way, I'm grateful that
I have You to turn to with my frustrations.
Thanks for always being there for me, Father.

Stuck in Traffic

• • • • • •

Thank You, Lord, for giving me this opportunity
to slow down and stop rushing through life.
Sometimes I need a reminder that it's okay if
things don't go my way. It's Your master plan that
really matters. I may arrive at my destination later
than intended, but I am grateful to have this time
to spend with You.

Road Construction

• • • • • •

Even though I may perceive road construction as a hassle, Lord, I am thankful for safe roads to drive on. Remind me that the big picture is worth all the detours and delays.

Red Lights and Stop Signs

• • • • • •

Lord, these delays aren't often welcome, but I know they are necessary to ensure my safety and the safety of everyone else on the road. Help me recognize these moments of pause as quick opportunities to reflect and recharge.

Praise the LORD; I may never forget the good things he does for me. He forgives all my sins and heals all my diseases. He redeems me from death and crowns me with love and tender mercies.

PSALM 103:2–4 NLT

Long To-Do List

• • • • • •

Dear Jesus, I am overwhelmed. There are many things on my list to do today. Thank You for giving me useful work to do, and I pray that Your priorities would be mine.

Tough to Get Out of Bed

• • • • • •

Lord, it seems the moment I settle in to sleep, the alarm goes off and it is time to face another day. Thank You for the hope and brightness of morning and the promise this new beginning brings.

Another Day on the Job

• • • • • •

Lord, thank You for this job. Though I don't
always look forward to it, it is a gift from You.
I am grateful for meaningful work to do and a
steady paycheck. Help me to be a light among my
co-workers.

Monday

• • • • • •

Father, thank You for a new week and a clean
slate. I don't always look forward to Mondays, but
I am grateful You have given me this day as an
opportunity to start new projects and finish old
ones. Help me be productive and consistently put
You first.

The LORD says, "I will guide you along the best pathway for your life. I will advise you and watch over you."

PSALM 32:8 NLT

A Day of Meetings

• • • • • •

Father, there are many ways I'd like to spend this day and sitting in meetings is not one of them, but thank You for sitting here with me. Thank You for a job that provides for my family. Thank You that all meetings eventually come to an end.

Working Late

• • • • • •

Father, it's hard to work late, but I'm thankful I have a job and work to do. Thank You for an opportunity to work without interruptions and for helping me meet this deadline.

New Responsibility

• • • • • •

Lord, I am grateful for being entrusted with this
new responsibility, even though it may mean
more work. Thank You for those people in my life
who trust me with important tasks. With Your
help, I know I won't let them down.

Change

• • • • • •

Lord, thank You for the constancy of change. I
may not always like it, but I know it's a necessary
part of life. Remind me that even when I think
things have changed for the worse, there is always
a blessing to be gained.

Godliness with contentment is great gain.

1 TIMOTHY 6:6 KJV

Home Sweet Home

The blessings at your doorstep

Telemarketers

• • • • • •

Lord, when I think of telemarketers, nothing
good comes to mind. Thank You for Your example
when it comes to dealing with people I don't like.
Though I may groan when the phone rings at
dinnertime, I will make a habit of looking to You
for guidance and patience.

Spiders in the Garden

• • • • • •

I am in awe of Your creation, Father, and there
are few things more exquisite than a dew-laden
spiderweb at dawn while I'm pulling weeds—
but when it comes to encountering the spiders
themselves. . .that's a different story. Help me
recognize the beauty and benefits in the creepiest
and crawliest of Your amazing creatures. I know
my garden would be at a loss without them.

First Dandelion

• • • • • •

Father, the first dandelion is a sure sign that spring is on the way, but I dread its appearance in my lawn. Thank You for this promise of new life, and remind me that You alone are the master of Your creation.

Bird Droppings on the Windshield

• • • • • •

Lord, sometimes it seems as though the birds know when I've just washed the car. Thank You for Your amazing creations that fly and sing so sweetly throughout the day. Help me keep my frustration in perspective.

This is the day the LORD has made;
let us rejoice and be glad in it.
PSALM 118:24 NIV

Walking the Dog

• • • • • •

Sometimes taking care of a pet can be a hassle, Lord, but I thank You for this fresh air—this time to get away from the phone, the television, and the doorbell. Thank You for the way this walk energizes me and gives me something productive to do.

Cleaning the Litter Pan

• • • • • •

It's not a task I look forward to, Father, but my feline companion is worth it. Thank You for all the joy the furry friends in my life bring.

Paying the Rent/Mortgage

• • • • • •

Father, thank You for a place to lay my head and
for the warmth and security my home provides.
Thank You for the resources that enable me to
write this check each month.

Hanging Pictures

• • • • • •

Lord, hanging pictures is sometimes tedious.
It can be a chore making sure things are straight
and properly placed. Thank You for the memories
these pictures hold. Thank You for being present
in all the details of my life.

All the days of the afflicted are bad,
but a cheerful heart has a continual feast.

PROVERBS 15:15 NASB

A Messy Closet

• • • • • •

Father, I am grateful to You for blessing me with the resources to have such a jam-packed closet. Though I dread cleaning it, guide me in keeping only what I need and donating the rest to those who are less fortunate. Thank You for always meeting my needs—spiritually and physically.

Making the Bed

• • • • • •

I never look forward to having one more thing to do in the morning, Lord, but I'm glad to have a warm bed to sleep in when I come home at night. Help me take pride in the blessings You have given me.

Brushing My Teeth

* * * * * *

Father, brushing my teeth often feels like just another thing on my morning and nightly to-do list. Though it can be a hassle, I'm grateful that I have access to the necessary resources to care for my body and for the daily opportunity to keep myself healthy.

Changing a Lightbulb

* * * * * *

Changing a lightbulb is such a simple thing but often something I put off and take for granted. Thank You for the blessing of light, and continue to guide me in seeking Your light.

Do not conform any longer to the pattern
of this world, but be transformed by
the renewing of your mind.

ROMANS 12:2 NIV

Washing Dishes

• • • • • •

Dishpan hands, murky water, stuck toiling away after dinner while everyone else goes about their business. . . Not much to love about washing dishes, Lord. I am grateful, though, for clean running water and being able to wash my dishes so thoroughly and conveniently.

On the Bathroom Scale

• • • • • •

The bathroom scale doesn't lie, Lord. You have blessed me abundantly and it shows. I am grateful for these few extra pounds—especially when I consider that there are so many less fortunate than me who go hungry every day. Show me how to provide for others as You have so generously provided for me.

Cleaning the Attic/Basement

• • • • • •

Thank You, Lord, for all the memories these boxes hold. As I sift through everything here, help me hang on to my fond memories and let go of the meaningless objects. I am grateful that You have blessed me with such a full life and rich legacy of loved ones.

Folding Laundry

• • • • • •

Father, sometimes the laundry seems never ending, but I'm glad this means plenty of clean clothes for me and my family. Thank You for blessing us with a convenient means of washing away the stains of the day and for providing us with clean hearts, too.

Do not be anxious about anything,
but in everything, by prayer and petition,
with thanksgiving, present your requests to God.
And the peace of God, which transcends
all understanding, will guard your hearts.

PHILIPPIANS 4:6–7 NIV

Pouring a Glass of Water

• • • • • •

Father, I turn on a faucet at least a dozen times
a day, never expecting anything but clean water
to come out. I'm grateful I've never had reason to
doubt this everyday blessing—or Your awesome
love for me. Thank You for the gift of faith.

Scrubbing the Toilet Bowl

• • • • • •

Lord, this is not a pleasant task, but I am forever
grateful for the sanitary conveniences I have
available to me. Thank You for blessing me with
a clean, healthy environment and the ability to
maintain it.

Cleaning the Chimney

• • • • • •

Lord, thank You for all the warm, comforting fires that made this chimney so dirty. I am grateful for Your gift of fire and the warmth of Your everlasting love.

Taking Out the Trash

• • • • • •

Even though this is one of my least favorite chores, Father, I am grateful that You have blessed my family with so many resources that we can afford to dispose of some of them. Help us keep Your creation bright and beautiful by making us mindful of what we throw away.

Offer unto God thanksgiving;
and pay thy vows unto the most High.

PSALM 50:14 KJV

Running a Bath

• • • • • •

Father, it sometimes seems like it takes forever for the bath to fill up—especially when I need one the most. Give me patience to wait for Your blessings. Thank You for abundant water and warm, bubbly relaxation.

Nothing on TV

• • • • • •

Thank You for this opportunity to spend time with my family and do something productive, Lord. I seem to be always seeking someone or something to entertain me. Thank You for blessing me with this free time to focus on others and grow closer to the ones I love.

Turning On the Lights

• • • • • •

Lord, thank You for the things I take for granted
every day, like electricity—the flip of a switch, and
my world is illuminated. Thank You especially for
the light You provide that guides my steps as I go
about my day.

Cutting the Grass

• • • • • •

Lord, there is nothing like the smell of freshly cut
grass. Thank You for fresh air and exercise. Thank
You for the beauty that surrounds me while I
work.

*Give thanks in all circumstances, for this is
God's will for you in Christ Jesus.*

1 THESSALONIANS 5:18 NIV

Computer Is Down

• • • • • •

Father, Your Word says to give thanks in all
circumstances, even when my computer is down.
Thank You for the time to quiet my soul and rest
my brain from the constant stream of information.

Deciding What to Fix for Dinner

• • • • • •

Father, in a world where so many are in need,
thank You for the luxury of wondering what to fix
for dinner. Thank You for the daily bread only You
can provide.

Cleaning the Kitchen

• • • • • •

Father, the kitchen is a mess and I'm tired, but thank You for the strength to clean it up. Thank You that messy kitchens (and lots of other messes in my life) are only temporary.

Shoveling Snow

• • • • • •

Father, thank You for the beauty of snow and for endowing me with the strength to move it from my path. Help me always recognize Your beautiful blessings—even if they require a little extra effort to adapt to.

*Why art thou cast down, O my soul? and
why art thou disquieted within me? hope thou
in God: for I shall yet praise him, who is the
health of my countenance, and my God.*

PSALM 42:11 KJV

Raking Leaves

• • • • • •

Thank You, Father, for the beauty of autumn—for the crisp air and fall colors. Thank You for this exercise and the opportunity to be outdoors. I am so grateful for Your blessings in due season.

Nosy Neighbors

• • • • • •

Thank You, Lord, for neighbors who care about what's going on in my life. I may not always appreciate their attention, but I'm grateful to have people living close by who are looking out for me and my family, just as I am grateful for Your watchful care from above.

Putting Away Christmas Decorations

· · · · · ·

Dear Lord, it is such a joy to celebrate Your Son's birth. Thank You for another holiday season to enjoy with my family and friends. Thank You for the memories associated with each item I am packing away for next year. Help me to treasure the things that You do.

Trying a New Recipe

· · · · · ·

Lord, thank You for this new recipe. Thank You for the food You've provided and the creativity with which I can prepare it day after day. Thank You for the rich variety and the joy of preparing food for my family and friends.

Cleaning the Gutters

• • • • • •

Father, there is truly no limit to Your blessings. Thank You for providing me with a roof over my head and protection from storms. I rejoice in all Your provisions, great and small.

Crayon on the Wall

• • • • • •

Lord, thank You for creative expression and child-hood innocence. Though my first instinct is to be frustrated, grant me an understanding and forgiving heart. Help me guide my children in expressing themselves in productive ways that honor You.

Leftovers for Dinner

• • • • • •

Father, I don't always look forward to leftover night, but I'm glad to have the night off from cooking. Thank You for making sure I have everything I need and then some. Help me use this nourishment to do Your will.

Putting Away Spring Clothing

• • • • • •

Dear Jesus, thank You for another season come and gone. I am in awe of the careful way You craft one day to the next in a seamless array of beauty and splendor. Help me recognize and appreciate the unique gifts each season has to offer.

May God give you more and more
mercy, peace, and love.
JUDE 2 NLT

The Little Things

Everyday unsung treasures

Chewing Gum

• • • • • •

Lord, I'm so grateful for the little refreshers You have brought into my life. When my spirit needs a quick pick-me-up, I know I can always turn to You. Thank You for refreshing me daily in mind, body, and spirit.

Leaving on Vacation

• • • • • •

Father, thank You for vacations! Thank You for blessing me with this opportunity to relax and gain perspective. Thank You for going with me when I step out of my regular routine. Help me to see You in a new and fresh way while I revel in Your glorious gift of rest.

Tomorrow

• • • • • •

Lord, I am forever glad that no matter what today brings, I can always rely on Your promise of a new day—whether here on earth or with You in heaven. Thank You for this comforting guarantee that sustains my daily hope.

Taking Pictures

• • • • • •

Lord, thank You for this little camera that captures the precious moments of my life. I'm grateful You have provided me a way to vividly remember the special people and places I hold dear. You are a great, wise, and wonderful God.

Every good and perfect gift is from above,
coming down from the Father of
the heavenly lights.

JAMES 1:17 NIV

Parades

· · · · · ·

Father, thank You for parades—for smiles, music, and fun. I have much to celebrate—this day and always. Thank You for the joy of celebration.

My Team Wins

· · · · · ·

Father, I know that winning isn't everything, but it sure is fun. Thank You for this victory, and help me be a gracious winner.

Singing in Church

• • • • • •

Father, thank You for the chorus of voices around
me and for blessing me with a voice to join in.
Remind me that You delight in hearing every
voice singing Your praises—even those that are a
little off-key.

Favorite Song on the Radio

• • • • • •

Father, thank You for this song, for the way it lifts
my spirits and brings back so many fond memories. I am so glad You brought music and rejoicing
into the world.

*Give thanks to the L*ORD*, call on his name;*
make known among the nations what he has
done.

PSALM 105:1 NIV

Decorating

• • • • • •

Father, You are a creative God who loves to celebrate. Thank You for sharing Your creativity with me and for the chance to share it with others.

Reflection in the Mirror

• • • • • •

Thank You, Lord, for making me fearfully and wonderfully in Your image. Help me look past the superficial things I may not like about myself to find Your Spirit shining within me.

Janitors

• • • • • •

Thank You, Father, for the men and women behind the scenes who humbly work so hard to keep things neat and sanitary. The world would be a much less beautiful place without them. Give them strength in their daily tasks, and help me honor them by cleaning up after myself.

First Cookout of the Season

• • • • • •

Lord, thank You for this simple pleasure: a pleasant evening outdoors and delicious food to share with friends and family. I am so grateful for Your everyday gifts that bring my loved ones together.

Devote yourselves to prayer,
being watchful and thankful.
COLOSSIANS 4:2 NIV

Finding the Perfect Gift

• • • • • •

Father, thank You for blessing me with the time and resources to find this perfect gift. I am grateful for the opportunity to show a loved one how much I care for them. And thank You for the innumerable perfect gifts You have given me—especially Your Son, Jesus.

New Baby

• • • • • •

Lord, I am humbled by this miracle of life. I am filled with hope for the future. Thank You for this reminder of Your phenomenal love.

Writing a Letter

• • • • • •

Father, I don't sit down to write letters very often, but thank You for the beauty of the written word and for giving me the ability to record my thoughts. Thank You for Your Word and the way it lifts my spirit. May it be written on my heart today and always.

Windshield Wipers

• • • • • •

Father, thank You for windshield wipers and the warmth inside my car as I drive through this rain. I don't know what I'd do without a means to see the path before me clearly. Thank You for always going before me and keeping all my paths clear— rain or shine.

Let every thing that hath breath praise the LORD. Praise ye the LORD.

PSALM 150:6 KJV

The Concept of Forever

• • • • • •

I rejoice in words like *everlasting* and *infinite*,
Father, because Your Word has assured me they
are real. Nothing can ever separate me from
You—not even death. Thank You for the promise
of spending an eternity under Your watchful care.

The Snooze Button

• • • • • •

How I take that extra five minutes for granted,
Lord! Thank You for those extra few moments of
rest before another hectic day begins. Help me
find time throughout the day to rejoice in all Your
generous blessings.

Band-Aids

• • • • • •

Thank You for this simple comfort, Father. When I hurt myself, I'm so glad I have a quick remedy to turn to. Though I know a Band-Aid won't heal me, it covers my wound and guards it from infection—just as You cover my sins and heal me from the inside out. I'm so thankful for Your loving care.

Seconds

• • • • • •

Lord, how amazing it is that while I'm planning my life out in months and years, You account for every single second of my day? Help me cherish each and every one now and always.

*A gift is as a precious stone in the eyes
of him that hath it: whithersoever it turneth,
it prospereth.*

PROVERBS 17:8 KJV

Seat Belts

• • • • • •

Father, thank You for the everyday safeguards in my life that give me a little extra peace of mind while I'm out and about. I'm forever grateful for Your care and protection.

Silence

• • • • • •

Thank You, Father, for the gift of peace and stillness. How often I take it for granted! Help me discover You in every quiet moment.

Tissues

• • • • • •

Lord, thank You for small comforts when I'm sick or sad. The little things always seem to matter most when I'm in need. When I don't have a tissue handy, thank You for always being there to dry my tears and heal my ills.

White-Out

• • • • • •

Lord, thank You for the ability to cover my mistakes and begin anew. I am grateful for Your promise of forgiveness and the opportunity to be made new again through Your Son, Jesus.

*For everything God has created is good,
and nothing is to be thrown away or refused
if it is received with thanksgiving.*

1 TIMOTHY 4:4 AMP

Looking at the Stars

• • • • • •

Dear Lord, thank You for the beauty of lights in the sky. Thank You for the promise that Your Son will return from heaven with a shout and that there will be a celebration like no other when He comes to earth. Thank You for infinite possibilities.

A Good Novel

• • • • • •

Father, thank You for this book to read. Thank You for the way I can see You whenever I look for You—even in fiction. I pray that this book will teach me something about You and the life You have given me to live.

Good News

· · · · · ·

Father, thank You for this good news! Thank You for every good gift that comes from You. Help me to stay faithful in the good times and to live my life with a grateful heart.

Second Chances

· · · · · ·

Thank You for the mercy of second chances: rebounds, the UNDO button on the computer, and Your generous forgiveness. I am grateful for the many times You have cleansed my heart and purified my spirit. Thank You for accepting me, Lord, imperfections and all.

Because your love is better than life,
my lips will glorify you.

PSALM 63:3 NIV

Surprises

• • • • • •

So many of Your blessings are wonderfully unexpected, Father. Thank You for finding me worthy of Your love—and for sending me Your gifts when You recognize that I am most in need.

Christmas Cards

• • • • • •

When I think of all the Christmas cards I've received, Father, I realize how truly blessed I am with friends and loved ones who care. Thank You for all the simple pleasures of the holiday season.

Spell-Checker

• • • • • •

Father, thank You for the fail-safes in my life that gently correct my mistakes. Thank You for Your wise discipline. Help me to focus on my strengths rather than my weaknesses.

Wrinkle-Free Clothing

• • • • • •

Father, thank You for this blessed time-saver! May I use the time I've saved to praise You for Your daily goodness and everyday miracles.

Then was our mouth filled with laughter,
and our tongue with singing: then said
they among the heathen, The LORD hath
done great things for them.

PSALM 126:2 KJV

Socks

• • • • • •

Lord, socks are such a simple blessing that I
barely worry when one goes missing in the dryer.
Thank You for the warmth and protection they
provide. Help me keep all Your gifts in perspective and never take any of them for granted—
from the ordinary to the extraordinary.

Rest Areas

• • • • • •

Father, thank You for designated areas of rest
while I am on the road. I can be in such a hurry
sometimes to go as fast and as far as I can. Help
me remember that it's important to honor Your
gift of rest no matter where I may be.

Day Planners

• • • • • •

Lord, thank You for organization that conquers chaos. As I script out my life from day to day, help me always remember that Your plans come first. May I never be too busy to do Your will.

Headlights

• • • • • •

Father, thank You for bright lights that guide me to my nighttime destinations. It's such a blessing to have my path illuminated in the darkness. May I always walk in Your light as I travel though life on my way to Your kingdom.

*Worship the L*ORD *your God, and his blessing*
will be on your food and water.

EXODUS 23:25 NIV

Security

• • • • • •

Father, thank You for metal detectors, security systems, law enforcement, and all the things that give me peace of mind when I am away from home or all by myself. The world can be a frightening place, but I'm grateful that You are with me always. With You, I truly have nothing to fear.

Long-Distance Phone Calls

• • • • • •

Lord, thank You for the ability to communicate with my faraway friends and family with ease. It's such a blessing to hear their voices by just pushing a few buttons. Help me remember to keep You at the top of my speed-dial list. I'm so very grateful that You're eager to hear from me, 24/7.

Hotel Bibles

• • • • • •

I am so thankful that Your Word is everywhere, Father. Guide readers as they open this Book, and lead them to the truth of Your unconditional love and amazing promise of salvation.

Lofty Dreams

• • • • • •

Father, thank You for giving me the ability to dream big and set lofty goals for myself. I know that by Your will, all things are possible. Thank You for including me in Your master plan and helping me see my dreams to fruition.

*From the fullness of his grace we have all
received one blessing after another.*

JOHN 1:16 NIV

Good Advice

• • • • • •

Lord, good advice is truly invaluable, and I'm so thankful for the friends and acquaintances You've brought into my life who have led me down the right paths—even when I wasn't very receptive to their wise counsel. Thank You for always being there to listen to my troubles and for blessing me with caring individuals who tell me what I need to hear—not always what I want to hear.

Coupons

• • • • • •

Lord, every little bit counts, and I'm grateful for all the small ways You help me provide for my family. Thank You for endowing me with wisdom and frugality.

Express Checkout

• • • • • •

Lord, thank You for constant blessings that I can always count on, like the express checkout line. On days when nothing seems to go right, I'm grateful for these time-saving conveniences that are always there for me.

Road Maps

• • • • • •

Father, thank You for detailed maps that show me exactly how to get to where I'm going as I travel from place to place. It's so good to have reliable directions at my fingertips. Thank You for providing me with a moral compass, too, as I navigate to my final destination: You.

The blessing of the LORD brings wealth,
and he adds no trouble to it.

PROVERBS 10:22 NIV

Naps

• • • • • •

Thank You for opportunities, Lord, to refresh and recharge. Help me use the energy I gain to ease the burdens of others who are tired and overworked.

Elastic Waistbands

• • • • • •

Father, thank You for flexibility—not only in the clothing that I wear but also in Your love for me. Even though I am sometimes full of sin, You are always able to wrap Your loving forgiveness snug around me. Thank You for Your one-size-fits-all kind of love.

Home-Cooked Meals

• • • • • •

Thank You for this meal cooked by loving hands, Lord. I am truly blessed by this food and the care that went into making it. Help use this nourishment for Your will.

Happily-Ever-After Endings

• • • • • •

Lord, I know life isn't a fairy tale, but I'm grateful for the hope found in happily-ever-after endings. Help me recognize all the good things You have blessed me with daily and stay focused on the big picture: the ultimate happy ending that You have promised me in heaven.

Oh that men would praise the LORD
for his goodness, and for his wonderful
works to the children of men!

PSALM 107:21 KJV

Stopping to
Smell the Roses

Refreshing detours from the beaten path

Passing a Cemetery

· · · · · ·

Lord, I am so grateful that no one walks the earth
or leaves it without Your knowledge. Thank You
for the people and stories represented by these
stones. Thank You for the ones that I hold dear.

Passing a Wedding

· · · · · ·

Thank You, Jesus, for the sacrament of marriage
and its personal illustration of Your love for the
church. Thank You for new beginnings and the
joy of celebration.

Garage Sales

• • • • • •

Father, compared to most of the world, we are wealthy beyond belief. We have so much stuff that even our garages are filled with items we no longer want or can use. Help me use my wealth wisely to honor You.

At the Mall

• • • • • •

Dear Lord, the people here represent so many different walks of life. Help me to see them through Your eyes and love them as You do. Thank You for the beauty of diversity and the breadth and depth of Your love for each of us.

The LORD has done great things for us,
and we are filled with joy.

PSALM 126:3 NIV

Voting

• • • • • •

Father, thank You for the opportunity to cast my vote. Though I may not always be motivated, I am grateful for the freedoms that come with living in a democracy. Help me make wise decisions concerning our leaders.

Making a Craft

• • • • • •

Lord, thank You for the gift of creativity. Thank You for giving me the time and ability to construct things with my hands. Help me bless someone with my creative endeavors today.

In a Crowd

* * * * * *

Father, I can see how people feel lonely in a crowd. Thank You for the companions You've given me on life's journey. Thank You that even in a crowd, I am uniquely loved by You.

Car Getting Repaired

* * * * * *

Lord, I'd rather not be getting my car repaired, but I am grateful that I will soon be able to travel safely again. Thank You for the mechanic who knows how to fix what's wrong. I pray that You would bless him as he helps service this vehicle on which I rely so much.

Be joyful in hope, patient in affliction,
faithful in prayer.

ROMANS 12:12 NIV

Stuck at a Railroad Crossing

• • • • • •

Heavenly Father, thank You for this time-out in my busy day to sit quietly and reflect. Thank You for the trains that bring us the things we need and take us where we want to go.

At the Library

• • • • • •

Lord, thank You for the silence in this place. Thank You for the bounty of books and endless shelves of reading material. Even though this place is rich with knowledge, help me always be mindful that You are wiser still.

Purchasing the Thanksgiving Turkey

• • • • • •

Lord, there are so many turkeys to choose from. Whether I want one that's big, small, roasted, or fried, I can have my choice. We are blessed beyond belief. Thank You for providing food for our nourishment and our pleasure.

A New Business Opens

• • • • • •

Lord, I see a new business has opened in my community. Thank You for the new hope and opportunity there. I pray that You would bless the owners and the employees and guide them in becoming a productive part of the community.

"I will send down showers in season;
there will be showers of blessing."

EZEKIEL 34:26 NIV

Waiting to See the Doctor

• • • • • •

Father, I am amazed at the intricacy and miracle of the human body. Thank You for the privilege of receiving quality medical care. Bless my doctors, and give them wisdom as they care for me.

Waiting for an Ambulance to Pass

• • • • • •

Lord, thank You for medical care that is readily available to us anytime we call. Thank You for the flashing lights and the urgency with which professionals respond to our needs. Protect and bless them on their way.

Waiting for a Restaurant Table

• • • • • •

Lord, I can become so impatient waiting for good things to come. Thank You for this special time away from home and the company of those I'm with. Help me stay positive and focused on the good things You have blessed me with right now.

Passing the Collection Plate

• • • • • •

Lord, thank You for the bountiful blessings You have bestowed on our church community. Thank You for the generosity of everyone around me. Help me to follow their example as I offer my contribution. May these tithes bring prosperity to our church and those in need.

*Thus you will be enriched in all things
and in every way, so that you can be
generous, and [your generosity as it is]
administered by us will bring forth
thanksgiving to God.*

2 CORINTHIANS 9:11 AMP

Volunteering

. . . . . .

I am so thankful for this opportunity to donate my time and energy to a worthy cause, Father. Thank You for giving me the perfect example of self-sacrifice in Your Son, Jesus. Guide me in making my actions speak louder than my words today.

Washing My Hands

. . . . . .

Lord, thank You for this simple act I take for granted. Thank You for the germ-cleansing power of soap and water and the spirit-cleansing power of Your love.

Pumping Gas

· · · · · ·

I always view this task as such a mundane one, Lord, but it's really a small miracle to have such abundant natural resources at my disposal. Thank You for always providing everything I need—I am forever grateful for Your awesome provisions.

Trying on Clothes

· · · · · ·

Father, thank You for so many options in dressing up my exterior appearance. Thank You for modest choices that flatter the figure You have blessed me with. Remind me continually that what's on the inside will always matter more to You than what's on the outside.

*Praise be to the God and Father of our
Lord Jesus Christ, who has blessed us
in the heavenly realms with every
spiritual blessing in Christ.*

EPHESIANS 1:3 NIV

At the Family Reunion

• • • • • •

Lord, help me rejoice in this time with my family today. Thank You for all the ups and downs we've shared together and our rich legacy of hope and trust in You. Thank You for sharing in this celebration with us today.

Another Birthday

• • • • • •

Lord, I don't always look forward to growing another year older, but I thank You for the opportunity to enjoy another year of Your bountiful blessings on earth. Thank You for parties and cake and thoughtful gifts. May I continue to live out my days as a witness to Your goodness.

During a Blackout

• • • • • •

Lord, thank You for the beauty of burning candles illuminating the darkness. Thank You for this time to rediscover how many of Your blessings we take for granted. Thank You for always looking out for us. Help us appreciate this quiet time as a way to strengthen our relationships with those around us.

Ordinary Days

• • • • • •

Father, help me treasure this uneventful day and realize how priceless it truly is. Thank You for another opportunity to learn, grow, live, explore, and love. Help me relish every moment as though it were my last.

*Have the roots [of your being] firmly
and deeply planted [in Him, fixed and
founded in Him], being continually built up
in Him, becoming increasingly more confirmed
and established in the faith, just as you were
taught, and abounding and overflowing
in it with thanksgiving.*

COLOSSIANS 2:7 AMP

Breaking in a New Pair of Shoes

• • • • • •

Lord, it's not always pleasant breaking in a new pair of shoes, but I'm grateful nonetheless for yet another provision. Guide me in these and all my steps down a path of service and goodwill that will glorify You.

Meeting Someone New

• • • • • •

Lord, thank You for allowing my path to cross with this new friend. Help me plant seeds of kindness in my new friend's life that will inspire her to know You better.

Coincidences

* * * * * *

Lord, thank You for happy coincidences and days
when things seem to just fall into place. Help me
always remember and recognize these moments
as examples of Your awesome power working in
my life. All credit goes to You for the good things
that come my way.

Pulling Weeds

* * * * * *

Father, thank You for the gift of gardening—for
the beautiful diversity of plants and flowers in
the world. I get so frustrated with the weeds that
invade my manicured space, but I know I should
be grateful for new life in all forms—no matter
how unwelcome they may be. Help me to live
in harmony with all Your creation and recognize
that You are the ultimate designer of landscapes.

*"Giving thanks is a sacrifice
that truly honors me."*
PSALM 50:23 NLT

Cleaning Up after a Party

• • • • • •

Lord, cleaning up isn't my favorite task, but I know it's a necessary one—especially when You've blessed me abundantly with good friends. Thank You for surrounding me with so many wonderful people. I am grateful for the daily richness they bring to my life.

Someone Honks at Me

• • • • • •

Lord, thank You for small reminders that I am not perfect. Help me be a polite and courteous driver, and guide me in recognizing other areas of my life where I could improve.

Windy Day

• • • • • •

Heavenly Father, although I cannot see it, I feel
the wind. You are a holy and awesome God—
even the winds and waves obey You. Thank You
for this tangible example of Your power.

Received a Favor

• • • • • •

Thank You for this gift, Lord. I feel so undeserv-
ing, yet You saw my need and sent someone to
respond. Thank You for seeing that all my needs
are met.

When I look at your heavens, the work of your fingers, the moon and the stars, which you have set in place, what is man that you are mindful of him, and the son of man that you care for him? Yet you have made him a little lower than the heavenly beings and crowned him with glory and honor.

PSALM 8: 3–5 ESV

Can't Sleep

• • • • • •

Father, even when I lie awake in the night, You are with me. Thank You for the rare silence and the opportunity to speak with You. Thank You for whispering to my heart—help my ears to hear You.

Anticipation

• • • • • •

Thank You for giving me this thing to look forward to, Father. I'm so excited that I can hardly wait! Help me recognize the little joys in each moment of my life, so I will look forward to living each and every second of the day with hope and enthusiasm.

Crossing the Street

• • • • • •

Lord, thank You for the safety of crosswalks, for laws, and for giving me a place to go. Help me dedicate all the small moments of my life to You.

Reading the Newspaper

• • • • • •

Lord, there is so much bad news in the world, but I am grateful that You make all things work for good. Thank You for freedom of speech, political diversity, and the refreshing humor of the comics. I pray Your master plan reigns supreme in my life.

"I will make you into a great nation and I will bless you; I will make your name great, and you will be a blessing. I will bless those who bless you, and whoever curses you I will curse; and all peoples on earth will be blessed through you."

GENESIS 12:2–3 NIV

A Light Load

• • • • • •

Father, You have given me such a good life. I've had my ups and downs, but all Your burdens are blessings in disguise. Thank You for giving me a light load to carry on my journey to You.

An Airplane Flies Overhead

• • • • • •

Lord, thank You for endowing man with the inspiration and wisdom to soar like a bird. You have blessed us with such staggering brainpower. Help us use it for good and in ways that will benefit all Your creation.

Passing a Farm

• • • • • •

You have blessed us with such abundant (and delicious!) resources, Lord. Thank You for bountiful harvests and for friends and loved ones gathered around my table.

Wrapping Gifts

• • • • • •

Father, thank You for these gifts to wrap. Thank You for my loved ones, who are the true gift. Help me to be a blessing to them as they have blessed me.

The LORD gave, and the LORD hath taken away; blessed be the name of the LORD.

JOB 1:21 KJV

Finding the
Silver Lining

Recognizing the good in everything

When My Faith Is Challenged

• • • • • •

Father, thank You for the truth of Your Word and for always providing me with a ready answer when I am questioned by those who haven't yet experienced the saving grace of Your Son. Thank You for this opportunity to be a light to the world—to share Your glorious promises with others and bring them closer to an understanding of Your unconditional love.

When My Heart Is Broken

• • • • • •

Lord, You are the healer of all things broken and despairing. Thank You for this opportunity to put things into perspective and grow in my relationship with You. I don't have much to offer, but I know that in Your loving embrace my tattered spirit will become new again.

A Full Medicine Cabinet

• • • • • •

Father, there are so many pills and bottles in my medicine cabinet that opening the door causes a veritable avalanche. But instead of focusing on the ills these medications treat, help me celebrate their healing qualities. Thank You for all the miracles of modern medicine, big and small.

Receiving a Disappointing Gift

• • • • • •

Lord, help me be thankful for every gift that comes my way—even if it's not what I wanted or was expecting. Big or small, expensive or thrifty, it is truly a blessing to receive gifts of any kind. Thank You for this thoughtful gesture and help me celebrate with genuine gratitude.

*You have turned for me my mourning
into dancing; You have loosed my sackcloth
and girded me with gladness.*

PSALM 30:11 NASB

Speeding Tickets

• • • • • •

Thank You for this reminder to slow down, Lord. This is a hard lesson to learn, and I'm not eager to accept the consequences of my actions—but with Your help, I know I can become a more conscientious driver and individual.

Stale Bread

• • • • • •

Father, thank You for blessing my family with so much food that we can't consume it quickly enough! Guide us in wasting fewer of Your precious resources, and help us use Your daily bread for Your will.

Gray Hair and Laugh Lines

• • • • • •

Aging isn't easy, Father, but I'm glad You have blessed me with a full life. Help me recognize these gray hairs and wrinkles as testaments to Your gifts of wisdom, laughter, and grace.

My Team Loses

• • • • • •

Lord, losing isn't fun. It's hard to put forth so much effort and to end in defeat, but help me see this loss in the light of eternity. Thank You that this loss is temporary and for the promise that You've won the only victory that matters.

*Our hearts ache, but we always have joy. We
are poor, but we give spiritual riches to others.
We own nothing, and yet we have everything.*

2 CORINTHIANS 6:10 NLT

Losing Something of Sentimental Value

• • • • • •

Father, this experience has taught me that things are just things—that what is most important in life is cherishing my relationship with You above all else. I may have lost part of a special memory today, but I know I can never lose You. Thank You for being with me forever and always.

The Check-Engine Light

• • • • • •

Dear Father, thank You for this little light that warns me of trouble. Though I may not acknowledge its appearance joyfully, I'm thankful that I can count on it to identify problems before any damage is done. Help me recognize the value of Your warnings and praise You for the consistency of Your love and care.

The Anniversary of a Loss

• • • • • •

Father, today is a sad day, and I am reminded of my loss. Thank You for the peace You bring to my soul and for the promise that weeping only lasts for the night and joy comes in the morning.

Eating Alone

• • • • • •

Lord, it's hard to be left out, but thank You that I am not truly alone. Thank You for Your presence and for the people I do have in my life. Thank You for caring for me when I feel that no one else does.

When you have eaten and are satisfied,
praise the LORD your God for the good
land he has given you.

DEUTERONOMY 8:10 NIV

Driving an Old Car

• • • • • •

Though I may dream about driving a shiny new car, Lord, I'm grateful for this one that has served me so reliably over the years. Give me a grateful heart, Father, and help me avoid coveting unnecessary luxuries.

Unused Sick Days

• • • • • •

Lord, thank You for keeping me well this year. I wish I could take advantage of more time off, but I know I need to be in the workplace, shining the light of Your Son's example into the lives of all those I encounter. Help me do productive work in Your name each and every day I am able.

Unanswered Prayers

• • • • • •

It amazes me, Father, how You know my needs so intimately. Thank You for listening to all my prayers—even the unreasonable ones—and providing me with comfort and direction. Your ways are mysterious, but I'm grateful that You always have the big picture in mind.

Sunburn

• • • • • •

Father, thank You for sunshine and warm, cloudless days. Sometimes I get so excited about rejoicing in the weather outdoors that I forget to protect my skin properly. Help me heal quickly so I can start enjoying the delicious warmth of summertime again soon.

In the day of prosperity be joyful, but in the day of adversity consider: Surely God has appointed the one as well as the other, so that man can find out nothing that will come after him.

ECCLESIASTES 7:14 NKJV

When I Forget an Umbrella

• • • • • •

Lord, give me a child's heart today, and help me rejoice in this rain. So what if I get a little wet? Thank You for puddles to jump in and rainbows after the storm.

Discipline

• • • • • •

Thank You, Father, for Your firm and consistent correction. I do not like to be disciplined, but I know it's for my own good. Open my mind, and help me face the consequences of my actions with dignity and humility.

When the Unexpected Happens

• • • • • •

Lord, thank You for unpredictability in life.
Though it's hard sometimes, I'm glad that only
You know what the future holds. Thank You for
allowing me to live one moment at a time.

When My Plans Fall Through

• • • • • •

Lord, let this disappointment be a reminder that
nothing in life is set in stone—except You. Thank
You for being there to uplift and comfort me
when all else is lost.

*Everything God created is good, and nothing is
to be rejected if it is received with thanksgiving.*

1 TIMOTHY 4:4 NIV

When I'm under Pressure

• • • • • •

Lord, thank You for all those who rely on me at home, at work, and in my daily life. It is a good feeling to be needed. Give me strength to fulfill my duties and obligations to the best of my ability. I leave the rest in Your capable hands, Father.

Embarrassment

• • • • • •

Lord, thank You for this humbling moment. I need reminders sometimes that I am only human. Thank You for loving and forgiving me in spite of myself.

Uncertainty

• • • • • •

I confess, Lord, that I do not like uncertainty. It is tempting to become anxious because I don't know how this is going to turn out. Thank You for being here with me and for holding my future so gently and carefully in Your loving hands. I know You will help me become a stronger person no matter the outcome.

Temptation

• • • • • •

Father, thank You for gracing me with the gift of free will. I am so grateful for Your trust in my ability to make my own decisions. Thank You for consequences that remind me of what's right and what's wrong. Give me a heart that strives for right. Though temptation can be hard to resist, I know it is fleeting. Only Your goodness will last an eternity.

"So do not fear, for I am with you; do not be dismayed, for I am your God. I will strengthen you and help you; I will uphold you with my righteous right hand."

ISAIAH 41:10 NIV

When I've Been Offended

• • • • • •

Jesus, my heart hurts, but I thank You for this
pain because it means I am alive and real. I know
that I will grow through this adversity. Help me
to forgive as You have forgiven me.

Bad News

• • • • • •

Lord, I know this news was not a surprise to You,
but it has caught me off guard. Thank You for
the promise that You can bring good out of every
situation—even the ones that seem very bad to
me. Help me trust You to see me through.

The GPS Fails

• • • • • •

When I'm lost, Father, my initial reaction is to feel frustrated and scared. Help me recognize the times I'm lost as opportunities to explore and discover new people, places, and things—new blessings. And when I stray too far off the beaten path, thank You for being the Good Shepherd who guides me back to where I belong.

Extreme Weather

• • • • • •

Father, thank You for the awesome power of Your creation. Though I may tremble in the face of storms, remind me that no storm lasts forever and that You are always cradling me securely in the palm of Your hand.

The LORD is my strength and my shield;
my heart trusts in him, and I am helped.
PSALM 28:7 NIV

Daylight Savings Time

• • • • • • •

Father, I dread losing an hour of precious sleep, but I know, like everything else, this, too, shall pass. Thank You for the blessing of sunshine and for giving us the wisdom to recognize our need for conservation. Thank You for all the little ways we are able to honor Your creation.

Losing a Job

• • • • • • •

Lord, thank You for this opportunity to explore the many spiritual and physical gifts You have bestowed on me. Help me overcome my feelings of abandonment and betrayal and open my mind to discover the rich possibilities that are all around me. Thank You for being my wellspring of hope in times of need.

Scars

• • • • • •

Lord, thank You for these reminders of the trials and hurts I have overcome. I am so grateful for the blessings of strength, healing, and hope You've brought into my life.

Hard Work

• • • • • •

Father, I am happy for this productive work You have given me to do. Thank You for the satisfaction that comes from a job well done and for giving me a strong, disciplined spirit.

*It is God's gift that all should eat and drink
and take pleasure in all their toil.*

ECCLESIASTES 3:13 NRSV

Scripture Index

Genesis
12:2–3 127

Exodus
23:25 89

Deuteronomy
8:10 141

Job
1:21 130

Psalms
8:3–5 124
28:7 153
30:11 135
32:8 29
37:23 14
42:11 55
50:14 49
50:23 121
63:3 83
103:2–4 26
105:1 68
107:21 98
107:29 23

118:24 37
126:2 86
126:3 103
150:6 74

Proverbs
10:22 95
15:15 40
17:8 77

Ecclesiastes
3:13 156
7:14 144

Isaiah
41:10 150

Ezekiel
34:26 109

John
1:16 92

Romans
12:2 43
12:12 106

2 Corinthians
6:10 138
9:11 112

Ephesians
1:3 115

Philippians
4:6 20
4:6–7 46

Colossians
2:7 118
4:2 71

1 Thessalonians
5:16–18 17
5:18 52

1 Timothy
4:4 . . . . .11, 80, 147
6:6 32

James
1:17 65

Jude
2. 60